Fluency

4

Voyager

Passport F

ISBN 978-1-4168-0668-4

Printed in the United States of America   08 09 10 11 12 13 DIG 9 8 7 6 5 4 3 2

Table of Contents

Fluency Practice

 Read the story to each other.

 Read the story on your own.

 Read the story to your partner again. Try to read the story even better.

 Questions? Ask your partner two questions about the story. Tell each other about the story you just read.

Timed Reading

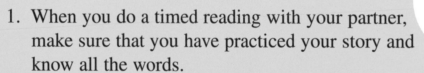

1. When you do a timed reading with your partner, make sure that you have practiced your story and know all the words.

2. When you are ready, tell your partner to start the timer.

3. Read carefully, and your partner will stop you at 1 minute. When you stop, mark your place.

4. Count the total number of words you read.

5. In the back of your Student Book, write the number of words you read and color in the squares on your Fluency Chart.

6. Now switch with your partner.

A Visit to the Big Apple

New York City is a thrilling city. It has many sites to see.

If you tour the city, start with the Empire State Building. This historic skyscraper is open to the public every day of the year. Go all the way to the top. On a clear day, you can see four other states.

Next, visit another tourist attraction, Ellis Island. This is the place where many immigrants first entered the United States. Its museum has many tapes and photos. (80) They tell the history of the place and the people who passed through there. The Statue of Liberty stands proudly and tall in the New York City Harbor. It is perhaps the most visited site in New York City.

You also may want to visit some of New York's museums. If you enjoy art, don't miss the Museum of Modern Art. It has many famous paintings and sculptures.

Finally, make sure you stop by Central Park. It covers almost a thousand acres. It has baseball diamonds, an ice-skating rink, horse carriage rides, playgrounds, and even a small zoo. (179)

A Small Price for an Island

New York City is one of the largest cities in the world. It has a population of more than 8 million people. The city is built on an island. What do you think this island looked like before it was covered with paved streets and tall buildings?

Native Americans were the first people to live on the island. They hunted and grew crops there. In 1609, Henry Hudson explored the area. He worked for a Dutch trading company. (78) The Dutch claimed the island, and a trading post was built. Dutch colonists began moving to the island. They named their settlement after a city back home. They called it New Amsterdam.

The colonists were eager to secure their claim on the land. They bought it from the Native Americans. They paid for it with small goods, such as knives and beads that were worth $24. That's a small price to pay for an island that would one day become famous! (159)

Hurry Up, Hank!

"Polly, would you take Hank to Jake's farm this morning?" Mother asked. Hank was one of the family's pigs. Polly was sure he was the most stubborn animal in the settlement.

"If you're back before noon," Mother said, "we can have lunch. Afterward, you may help me gather horsetail rushes."

"I'd love to," Polly answered, "if Hank cooperates, that is." Of all Polly's chores, gathering rushes was her favorite. (69) Horsetail rushes were used during colonial times for scouring or cleaning pots. Polly loved going to the marshes to find them.

An hour later, Polly stood in the middle of the road, her hands on her hips. Hank sat in the road. He refused to budge, even for passing colonists. "All right, Hank," Polly warned, "in 2 minutes, I'm going to start singing." Polly's family teased her about her shrill singing voice.

All of a sudden, Hank looked nervous, as if he understood this declaration. He got to his feet and ran all the way to Jake's farm. (167)

The Statue of *Liberty*

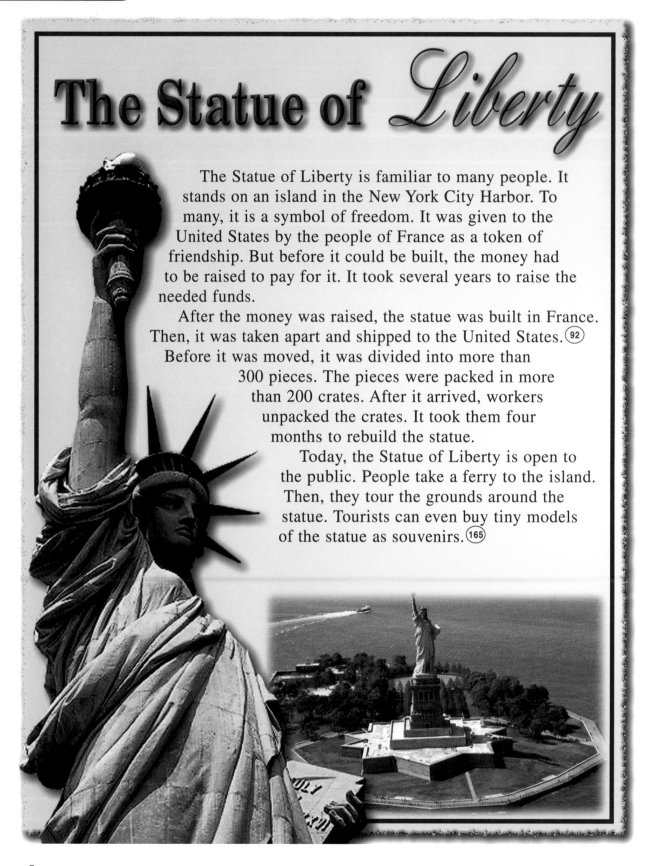

The Statue of Liberty is familiar to many people. It stands on an island in the New York City Harbor. To many, it is a symbol of freedom. It was given to the United States by the people of France as a token of friendship. But before it could be built, the money had to be raised to pay for it. It took several years to raise the needed funds.

After the money was raised, the statue was built in France. Then, it was taken apart and shipped to the United States. (92) Before it was moved, it was divided into more than 300 pieces. The pieces were packed in more than 200 crates. After it arrived, workers unpacked the crates. It took them four months to rebuild the statue.

Today, the Statue of Liberty is open to the public. People take a ferry to the island. Then, they tour the grounds around the statue. Tourists can even buy tiny models of the statue as souvenirs. (165)

A Search for Tickets and Maps

As Sam and his mom hopped off the bus and walked into the library, Sam's mom asked, "Would you like to help plan our weekend in New York City?"

"Sure!" said Sam. He sat down at the computer and typed *New York City* as a keyword search. Several Web sites came up. He clicked on one that looked like it really would help tourists. "Mom, did you know New York City has a huge population?" asked Sam.

"You thought Philadelphia was big, but New York City is much larger.⁸⁹

Let's preview a few of the museum Web sites," she said.

Sam clicked through a few more pages. They decided to go to the American Museum of Natural History. There was a space exhibit that looked interesting. Then, they looked for tickets to a Yankees' game. "We could take public transportation from the museum to the stadium," he said.

Finally, Mother said, "Let's print out a map that will help us tour Broadway." Looking at the city map, Sam said, "I feel like a tourist already. Don't you?"¹⁷⁷

Give Blood!
A Public Service Announcement

When was the last time you gave a gift to the people living in your community? If you wonder how you can help others, you might consider giving blood.

You probably know that blood saves lives. But did you know that when a person needs blood, nothing else will do? Nothing else can be used in the place of blood.

About 60 percent of the population qualifies to give blood. However, only about 5 percent of people take the time to help. (82) When you consider that someone needs blood every 2 seconds, you can understand the problem.

You can make a choice to be a part of the solution. There are two ways for you to register to give blood at the blood bank. The first way is to visit our Web site and sign up online. The second way is simply to call us. However, if you are in a hurry, go to the Web site. Our phone lines often are busy.

Come in today! We will show our appreciation with a cup of juice from Just Juices. (179)

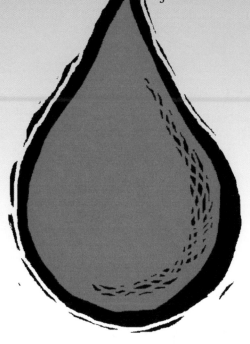

From the Blood Bank to the Hospital

Giving blood doesn't take long, and it helps many people. When you go to a blood bank, you give about one pint of blood. This only takes about 10 minutes. That pint of blood can help three people.

What happens to your blood after you give it? First, it is sent to a lab where special equipment separates it into three parts. These parts are red blood cells, platelets, and plasma.

The red blood cells help people who have lost blood. These cells must be used within about 40 days or frozen for later use. (95)

The platelets help people who cannot make enough of their own platelets because of illness. Platelets can be stored only for five days.

Plasma is the liquid part of the blood. It can be frozen and stored for a longer period of time.

Each unit of your blood is kept at the proper temperature until it is shipped to a hospital. Then at the hospital, the blood is matched with a patient. Only two days after you leave the blood bank, your blood may be helping someone heal. (183)

What Does Blood Do?

Blood carries oxygen, food, blood cells, and waste products through the body. About half of the volume of blood is made up of blood cells.

There are three kinds of blood cells—red blood cells, white blood cells, and platelets. This composition helps the different parts of the blood work together.

There are more red blood cells than any other kind. As these cells pass through the lungs, they pick up oxygen. The blood carries oxygen to the heart. From the heart it passes through the arteries, which extend to all parts of the body. ⑨⑤ As the blood moves through the body, different tissues absorb some of the oxygen. The tissues also release a waste gas into the blood. This gas is called carbon dioxide.

There are fewer white blood cells than other kinds of blood cells. White blood cells help the body fight disease and infection.

Platelets are smaller than red blood cells or white blood cells. These cells can stick together to form blood clots. When a person begins to bleed, blood is exposed to air and clots form. Then, the bleeding stops, and the body can repair the injured tissue. ⑲③

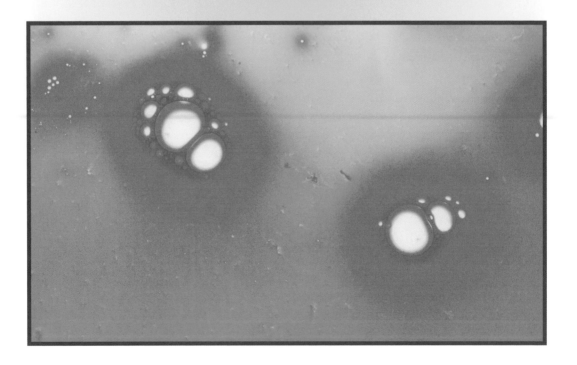

A Blood Bank on *Wheels*

"Marisa, could you help out on the blood van on Tuesday or Wednesday?" Mom asked. "Either day works for me, so it's your choice."

Marisa looked surprised. Their small community had gotten a new blood van the previous year. The van traveled to offices, libraries, and other locations in the area. This allowed people who could not get to blood banks to give blood.

Marisa's mother, who was a nurse, often volunteered on the blood van. For weeks, Marisa had been asking if she could help too. "Of course you can help," she replied. (94)

Marisa and her mother arrived at the blood van early. Inside, it looked like a doctor's office with equipment for drawing blood. Marisa learned that her job was to give a form to everyone who came. She also would check that each form was filled in correctly.

After working for three hours, Marisa and her mother were ready to go home. Marisa's mother gave Marisa a big hug. "That's to show my appreciation for all your help," she said.

Marisa smiled and said, "I should thank you. I had a wonderful time!" (186)

Alexander's Choice

Alexander heard a loud crack as his bat met the ball and sent it soaring. After running as fast as he could all the way to third base, he watched his best friend walk up to home plate. "Hit a home run, Russell!" he yelled.

Several minutes later, the game was tied, and Alexander ran to the water fountain to get a quick drink. The cool liquid refreshed him, but when he turned, he tripped and fell. His hand hit a rock and started bleeding.

Alexander's coach ran up to him and looked at his injured hand. (97)

"Let's go to the community center and get the first-aid kit," he said. "You'll heal quickly if we apply a bandage."

A few minutes later, the coach opened a box and laughed. "It looks like you have a choice," he said. "You can have either an orange bandage with green stripes or one that has a rabbit on it."

"I guess I'll take the one with the rabbit on it," Alexander answered. "Rabbits supposedly bring good luck, and I think the team will appreciate the help!" (184)

The White House Easter Egg Roll

Don't miss the White House Easter Egg Roll! This celebration, which dates back to 1878, is held every year at the White House. Children 6 years old and younger can join in the fun.

Many entertaining activities are planned. Children can meet story characters and listen to children's books read aloud. The most popular activity is the egg race. For this event, children run a race while trying to hold an egg in a spoon. (75)

The Easter Egg Roll will take place on the day after Easter. It will be held on the South Lawn of the White House. The event is free to the public. However, you must have a ticket to join some of the activities.

Pick up your tickets at the Visitor Center. The opening ceremony begins at nine in the morning. The Egg Roll will not be held if it rains.

To discover more about this fun event, please visit our Web site. (157)

Earth Day

Forty years ago, Gaylord Nelson began to worry about our planet. He saw clouds of smog in the air and pollution in our rivers. He knew that plants and animals were dying. He decided to do something to help the environment. He began by talking to our nation's leaders. They agreed it was time for a change. They discussed what could be done to help. Even so, few people took action to change things.

Nelson knew that he had to think of another way to help. He decided to have a special celebration to honor Earth. ⑨⑥ This day would be called Earth Day. It would be held each year in April. People would gather to learn what they could do to protect the planet.

Nelson's idea worked. In fact, the success of his idea was astounding. People promised to clean up the environment. They had fun too. Entertaining events were planned at Earth Day festivals throughout the nation.

Earth Day has been remembered every year since 1970. Many generations have enjoyed it. Word about Earth Day has spread. Now this day is popular, and people around the world celebrate it. ⑲⓪

Replogle 4.2 inch
POLITICAL GLOBE

LEGEND
National Capitals
Other Cities
Statute Miles
Kilometers
International Boundaries
State/Province Boundaries

Music, Food, and Fun

"It's time to go to the Cinco de Mayo celebration," Aunt Maria said happily. "Bring your sweater because it's chilly today."

It was Sue's first time to enjoy Cinco de Mayo in Mexico, the country where the holiday started. Sue had visited her aunt before, but never on the fifth day of May, the day of the holiday. Sue knew that it honored the courage of the Mexican people during a battle against the French army long ago.

They passed beautiful old buildings as they walked toward the town square. When they arrived, Sue could hear children playing and a choir singing. (102)

The smell of spicy foods filled the air. Girls danced in costumes and wore brightly colored bows in their hair. The boys wore red scarves around their necks. Red, white, and green flags waved in the breeze.

Sue and her aunt stayed at the festival for three hours. They sampled delicious snacks, listened to music, and watched a ceremony to honor the day. But the best part of the festival happened at home. That's when Sue and her aunt had a special conversation. "I hope you can come visit again next May," her aunt said.

"I do too!" Sue replied. (202)

A Gift for Mother's Day

As Stephen walked home, he sighed just as Mr. Harrison walked by. "Hey, Stephen," Mr. Harrison said cheerfully, "you look a little down. What's the problem?"

"Hello," Stephen replied. He enjoyed talking to Mr. Harrison, who worked in the neighborhood hardware store. "Mother's Day is two days away, and I don't even have an idea for a present."

"Why don't you come to the shop with me?" Mr. Harrison suggested. "I know we can find something for her." (78)

Stephen wondered what they could find for his mother in a store full of chainsaws and nails, but he was willing to try. As they entered the store, Mr. Harrison asked, "Does your Mom still like to paint?"

"She loves to paint," Stephen answered excitedly. "In fact, she's working on an astounding painting that's as big as that wall," he said, pointing to the back wall of the store. "The painting has an entertaining subject—our new puppy, Wolf."

In that instant, Stephen knew what he wanted to get for his mother. "Does your store carry paintbrushes?" he asked. "Mom likes to use big ones, the kind used for painting houses." (189)

The Birth of Memorial Day

You probably know that Memorial Day is a holiday. Yet you may not realize that it is not a day of celebration. Instead, it is a day for remembering. We honor people who have fought and died for our nation.

The holiday began at the end of the Civil War. A man in the South wanted to honor those who had lost their lives in that war. He planned a special event in May, and many people came. They sang songs and prayed. They placed flowers on soldiers' graves. (89)

A year later, another ceremony was held in May, this time in New York. The people of a small town took the day off. They watched a parade and placed flowers on graves. Flags were flown at half-staff. About 10 years later, New York became the first state to make the day a holiday.

Since then, many generations have celebrated Memorial Day.

After World War I, the purpose of Memorial Day changed. It became a time to remember soldiers from all wars. Today, the holiday is observed on the last Monday in May. (183)

Don't Miss Butterfly Camp!

Have you considered what our world would be like without butterflies? If you love butterflies, you won't want to miss Butterfly Camp next Saturday. You'll have a lot of fun while learning about these remarkable insects. Children from ages 9 to 13 are invited.

The goal of the camp is to teach people to appreciate nature. You'll learn why butterflies, like all insects, are important to our planet.

We'll begin our day with a walk in the garden. There, you'll see the kind of plants that attract butterflies. (88) Thousands of butterflies will flutter around your head like colorful raindrops. We'll look at the shapes and colors of their wings. Also, we'll observe their different flight patterns.

Next, we'll create artworks. You'll be able to draw or paint pictures of butterflies. Some of you may want to create a poster to show what you've learned. Then, you can decorate your walls at home with your art.

We'll end the day with a treat. We'll make real nectar for you to sample by mixing sugar, water, and food coloring. Then, you can discover what butterflies like best! (185)

A Caterpillar's Journey

Marta gazed outside her window. She saw a caterpillar with black and yellow stripes inching up the branch of a tree. Marta moved near it so she could observe it more closely.

Marta's father joined her. "It looks like it's really struggling," he said. "But soon it'll be able to fly away."

"Caterpillars can't fly," Marta said with a grin.

"It'll be a caterpillar for only a couple of weeks," Dad said. He reminded Marta that the caterpillar had started out as an egg and would end up as a butterfly. "It's in its larval stage now," he said. Then, he pointed out the window and said, "See that green thing?" (111)

Marta looked carefully and gasped. A tiny green cocoon with gold specks was hanging from the branch. "I remember now," Marta said. "That's what the caterpillar becomes next, a pupa."

"That's right," Dad replied. "It will be a pupa for about two weeks. If we keep an eye on it, we probably can watch it turn into a butterfly."

Marta stopped to consider this and then made a decision. She would draw a chart showing this remarkable cycle. She got some art supplies and began making simple sketches of the caterpillar. (202)

A New Set of Antlers

Have you ever seen a picture of a giant elk with huge antlers? Did you know that the antlers are shed each spring? When the old antlers are shed, the elk begins to grow a new, even larger set.

The new growth begins in early summer. First, two stems appear under the thin skin on the elk's head. This skin is called velvet. It is covered with tiny, soft hairs.

While they are growing, new antlers are very soft and can be injured easily. (84) Luckily, they are equipped with tiny feelers, or sensitive velvet hairs. The elk gently brushes the antlers against objects such as trees. This allows it to feel how large the antlers are and avoid hurting them.

By the end of the summer, the elk's appearance has been altered by a new set of antlers. You can tell how old an elk is by observing the size of its antlers. A young elk's first antlers are small. However, an adult elk may have antlers that are 4 or 5 feet long. It uses these antlers to attract females and defend its territory. (185)

Tracking Striped Bass

Most fish live in either salt water or freshwater. Striped bass are different. They live in salt water, but they move into freshwater to spawn, or lay eggs. Scientists know that some striped bass migrate great distances to spawn. They also know that some return to the same place each year.

In the past, scientists put tags on the fish to track their movements. They would release the tagged fish, wait a year, and catch them again. They put the information in charts, which helped them learn more about bass migration. (91) For example, they learned that some bass travel for remarkable distances. One fish traveled all the way from North Carolina to Maine.

However, this tagging system had problems. Sometimes scientists found a fish in the same place two years in a row. They couldn't tell if the fish had migrated. After considering possible solutions, they came up with an idea. They now use tags that send out constant sounds so scientists can follow the fish as they swim. These tags give them a better idea about what the bass are doing. It also helps them make decisions about how to protect this species. (194)

How a Flounder Becomes Flat

The Baby Flounder

Think of the last cartoon you saw with a cute fish character in it. That could be what a flounder looks like when it first comes out of its egg. Like most fish, it has fins, gills, and one eye on either side of its body. However, before it becomes an adult, the baby fish will face remarkable changes in the same way that a caterpillar in a cocoon does.

Big Changes

A few days after birth, the baby flounder, also called a flatfish, begins to change. In fact, it begins to become just that—flat! ⑨⑨ First, the baby fish begins to lean slightly to one side. Then, the eye on that side of its head begins to move! After awhile, the eye will have moved completely to the other side of the fish, next to the other eye. As the fish's eye moves, its bones, nerves, and muscles also begin to change. Even the color of the flounder changes. The "blind" side of the fish becomes pale.

The Adult Flounder

Finally, the flounder becomes an adult. It drifts to the bottom of the ocean and blends with its surroundings. With its two eyes it watches the scene above. ⑳⑫

Yellowstone National Park

In 1872, members of Congress were shown photos and paintings of a place in the West. They saw pictures of tall mountains and vast forests. Amazed by the region's beauty, they decided to preserve it as a park. It is called Yellowstone National Park. It is the oldest national park in the country.

Visitors to this immense park hike on mountain trails and swim in clear lakes. They watch wildlife and take photos of nature. But most agree that the most fabulous sights in the park are the geysers. A geyser occurs when hot water and steam shoot out of the ground straight into the air. (106)

Geysers form in places where the melted rock deep in the earth rises toward the surface. The hot rocks heat the water in channels under the ground. The water begins to boil and expand. Pressure builds up. Then, steam and water explode into the air.

Most of the world's geysers are located in Yellowstone. One of the most famous is called "Old Faithful." People who have seen Old Faithful erupt generally say that they will never forget the sight. Some also say thanks to the people who preserve the park. (196)

Almost Lost:
The Story of the Bison

In the early 1800s, many settlers traveled across the Great Plains. A few wrote letters back home to their loved ones. Some described a fabulous sea of grass rippling in the wind. Others wrote about herds of buffalo that stretched as far as the eye could see. At that time, there were tens of millions of buffalo, or bison.

Years later, only about 20 bison remained on Earth. This small herd was found in Yellowstone National Park soon after the park was established. Hunters had killed most of the other bison.(91) Later, Congress passed a law against hunting bison. But generally, the law did not help much. Ten years after it was passed, the herd was still very small.

A man who worked with a zoo in New York viewed this problem as a challenge. Along with others, he formed a group to help the bison. The group moved bison raised on ranches to special preserves. There, they could begin to adapt to life in nature. Later, they were placed back into the wild. Over time, the bison herds grew larger. Today, there are about 2,000 bison in Yellowstone.(189)

Word List

public	appreciation
famous	absorb
settlement	tissue
afterward	promised
tiny	festival
choice	choir